YOU CAN TRUST

THE BIBLE

Discovery House
P U B L I S H E R S
BOX 3566 · GRAND RAPIDS. MI 49501

*PUBLISHING BOOKS THAT FEED
THE SOUL WITH THE WORD OF GOD.*

YOU CAN TRUST

THE BIBLE

John R. W. Stott

CONTENTS

Preface

The substance of this little book was given as a series of five sermons in All Souls Church, Langham Place, London. I am grateful to Michael Baughen, then Rector of All Souls, for inviting me to preach them; to Inter-Varsity Press for suggesting that they should be written up for publication; to Mark Labberton, my former Study Assistant, for working through the first draft and making a number of helpful suggestions; and to Vivienne Curry for typing the final draft.

Although I have striven to eliminate the more obvious sermonic touches, and have elaborated some points that (owing to the constraints of the pulpit) were skimpy, yet the material remains substantially what it was when first delivered. The book's origin as sermons explains some of its characteristics. Each chapter seeks to expound a biblical text. There are no footnotes. The style is colloquial rather than literary. And the readership I have had in mind is similar to the composition of the All Souls church family, namely students and other thoughtful lay people, who want to think seriously about the authority and relevance of the Bible.

The book claims, therefore, to be no more than introductory. Important questions that are being discussed in scholarly circles today—questions, for example, about the meaning of language, the influence of culture, the sociology of knowledge, and the perception of truth—are hardly raised here. For this is a basic book about the historic Christian attitude toward Scripture, and about the Bible's own understanding of itself, which need to be restated in every generation, and which remain the essential perspective from which to grapple with other pressing problems.

The biblical text quoted is from the New International Version. However, occasional reference is made to the Authorized Version, and those passages are marked (AV).

John Stott

Introduction

Let me make a few preliminary points.

First, I imagine we all know that the Bible continues to be a world best-seller. I am told that the Koran has now been translated into more than 125 languages. But the whole Bible has been translated into 307 languages, the New Testament into 680 more, and at least one book of the Bible into 1,360 more. This makes a total of 2,347 languages and dialects into which some major portion of the Bible has been translated. In 1989 the United Bible Societies distributed 667 million copies of the Bible and Bible portions, and the total world sales by all publishers must run into the billions. Why? Why does this old book remain at the top of the charts?

Second, and paradoxically, this much purchased book is a much neglected book. Probably tens of thousands of people who buy the Bible never read it. Even in churches, knowledge of the Bible is abysmal. Forty years ago Cyril Garbett, the then Archbishop of York, wrote that "the majority of men and women neither say their prayers, except in some terrifying emergency, nor read their Bibles, unless to look for help in a crossword puzzle, nor enter a church from one end of the year to the other, except for a baptism, a marriage or funeral." And if that was true forty years ago, it is even more true today. Few parents read the Bible to their children, let alone teach them out of it. Few church members make a practice of daily Bible meditation. Few preachers wrestle conscientiously with the biblical text so as to grasp both its original meaning and its contemporary application. And some church leaders are brash enough publicly to express their disagreement with its plain doctrinal or ethical teaching. It is a tragic situation. What can be done to remedy it?

My third introductory point concerns the conviction that the Bible is a book, indeed *the* book, you can trust. A recognition of its unique inspiration and consequent authority has until quite recently been part of the historic faith of all Christian churches. Certainly submission to the authority of the Scripture, or, as I think we should express it better, submission to the authority of God as it is mediated to us through Scripture, has always been and still remains a major hallmark of evangelical Christians. We believe its instruction. We embrace its promises. We seek to obey its commands. Why so? Mainly because we believe the Bible is the Word of God, but also because He speaks to us through it with a living voice. The Bible was the book for yesterday. Without doubt it will be the book for tomorrow. But for us it is the book for today. It is God's Word for today's world.

So then, its continuing popularity, its regrettable neglect, and its contemporary relevance are three good reasons why we should give our minds to the book we can trust: the Bible.

1. God and the Bible

Our first topic, "God and the Bible," introduces us to the subject of revelation. For this my text is Isaiah 55:8-11. God Himself is speaking:

> "My thoughts are not your thoughts,
> neither are your ways my ways," declares the LORD.
> "As the heavens are higher than the earth,
> so are my ways higher than your ways
> and my thoughts than your thoughts.
> As the rain and the snow come down from heaven,
> and do not return to it without watering the earth and
> making it bud and flourish,
> so that it yields seed for the sower and bread for the eater,
> so is my word that goes out from my mouth:
> It will not return to me empty,
> but will accomplish what I desire
> and achieve the purpose for which I sent it."

From this great text there are at least three important lessons to learn.

The reasonableness of revelation

Some people find the very concept of revelation difficult. The idea that God should disclose Himself to mankind strains their credulity. "Why should He?" they ask, "and how could He?" My response is that the evident necessity of divine revelation makes the notion eminently reasonable. Most people in every age have felt baffled by the mysteries of human life and human experience. So most people have admitted that they need wisdom from outside themselves if they are ever to fathom the meaning of their own being, let alone the meaning of the being of God, if indeed there is a God. Let me take you right back to Plato. He speaks in the *Phaedo* about our having to sail the seas of darkness and doubt on the little "raft" of our own understanding, "not without risk," he adds, "as I admit, if a man cannot find some word of God which will more surely and safely carry him."

Without revelation, without divine instruction and direction, we human beings feel ourselves to be like a boat drifting rudderless on the high seas; like a leaf that is being tossed helplessly by the wind; like a blind person groping in the darkness. How can we find our way? More important, how can we find *God's* way without His direction? The impossibility of human beings discovering God by their own unaided intellect is very plainly asserted in verses 8 and 9 of my text. " 'My thoughts are not your thoughts, neither are your ways my ways,' declares the Lord. 'As the heavens are higher than the earth, so are my ways higher than your ways and my thoughts than your thoughts.' " In other words, there is a great gulf fixed between God's mind and human minds. The text expresses a contrast between the ways and the thoughts of God on one hand, and the ways and thoughts of human beings on the other. That is, between what we think and do, and what God thinks and does, there is this great chasm. The thoughts and ways of God are as much higher than the thoughts and ways of man as the heavens are higher than the earth; that means infinity.

Consider God's thoughts. How can we discover His thoughts or read His mind? Why, we can't even read each other's thoughts. We try to. We look into each other's faces to see if they are smiling or frowning. We peer into each other's eyes to see whether they're flashing or twinkling or somber or bright. But it is a risky business. If I stood here in the pulpit silent, and maintained a poker-face, you wouldn't have the foggiest notion what I was thinking about. Try. Let me stop talking for a few moments. Now, what was going on in my mind? Any guesses? No? Well, I'll tell you. I was scaling the steeple of All Souls Church, trying to reach the top! But you didn't know. You hadn't the faintest notion what I was thinking. Of course not. You can't read my mind. If we are silent, it is impossible to read one another's minds.

How much less possible is it (if indeed there are degrees of impossibility) to penetrate into the thoughts of Almighty God? His mind is infinite. His thoughts tower above our thoughts as the heavens tower above the earth. It is ludicrous to suppose that we could ever penetrate into the mind of God. There is no ladder by which our little minds can climb up into His infinite mind. There is no bridge that we can throw across the chasm of infinity. There is no way to reach or to fathom God.

It is only reasonable to say, therefore, that unless God takes the initiative to disclose what is in His mind, we shall never be able to find out. Unless God makes Himself known to us, we can never know Him, and all the world's altars—like the one Paul saw in Athens—will bear the tragic inscription, "TO AN UNKNOWN GOD" (Acts 17:23).

This is the place to begin our study. It is the place of humility before the infinite God. It is also the place of wisdom, as we perceive the reasonableness of the idea of revelation.

The way of revelation

Granted that it is reasonable for God to reveal Himself, how has He done so? In principle, in the same way that we reveal or disclose ourselves to one another, that is, by both works and words, by things we do and say.

Creative art has always been one of the chief means of human self-expression. We are conscious that there is something inside us that has to come out, and we struggle to bring it to birth. For some people the appropriate medium is music or poetry; for others one of the visual arts—drawing, painting or photography, pottery, sculpture, carving or architecture, dance or drama. It is interesting that of these artistic media pottery is the one most frequently used of God in Scripture—presumably because the potter was a well-known figure in the villages of Palestine. So God is said to have "formed" or "fashioned" the earth, and mankind to dwell upon it (e.g., Gen. 2:7; Ps. 8:3; Jer. 32:17). Moreover, He Himself is seen in His works. "The heavens declare the glory of God; and the firmament sheweth his handiwork" (Ps. 19:1, AV; Isa. 6:3). Or, as Paul writes near the beginning of Romans, "What may be known about God is plain to them [i.e., the Gentile world], because God has made it plain to them. For since the creation of the world God's invisible qualities—his eternal power and divine nature—have been clearly seen, being understood from what has been made" (Rom. 1:19-20). In other words, just as human artists reveal themselves in their painting, sculpture, or music, so the divine artist has revealed Himself in the beauty, balance, intricacy, and order of His creation. From it we learn something of His wisdom, power, and faithfulness. This is usually referred to as "natural" revelation, because it has been given in and through "nature."

It is not to this that my text refers, however, but rather to the second and more direct way in which we make ourselves known to one another, and God has made Himself known to us, namely through *words.* Speech is the fullest and most flexible means of communication between two human beings. I mentioned earlier that if I remained silent and poker-faced in the pulpit, I would be inscrutable to you and you could not discover what was going on in my mind. But now the situation has changed. Now you do know what is going on in my mind, because I am no longer silent. I'm speaking, I am clothing the thoughts of my mind in the words of my mouth. The words of my mouth are conveying to you the thoughts of my mind.

Speech, then, is the best means of communication, and speech is the main model used in the Bible to illustrate God's self-revelation. Look back at my text—verses 10 and 11: "As the rain and the snow come down from heaven, . . . watering the earth and making it bud and flourish, so that it yields seed for the sower and bread for the eater, so is my word . . . ." Notice the second reference to heaven and earth: It is because the heavens are higher than the earth that the rain comes down from heaven to water the earth. Notice also that the writer goes straight from the thoughts in the mind of God to the words in the mouth of God: "So is my word that goes out from my mouth: it will . . . accomplish what I desire and achieve the purpose for which I sent it." The parallel is plain. As the heavens are higher than the earth, but the rain comes down from heaven to water the earth, so God's thoughts are higher than our thoughts, but they come down to us, because His word goes out from His mouth and thus conveys His thoughts to us. As the prophet has said earlier, "the mouth of the LORD has spoken" (Isa. 40:5). He was referring to one of his own oracles, but he described it as a message coming out of the mouth of God. Or as Paul wrote in 2 Timothy, "All Scripture is God-breathed" (the literal translation of *theopneustos* in 2 Tim. 3:16). That is, Scripture is God's Word, issuing from God's mouth.

Having made the affirmation that my text expresses, it is important for me to add a couple of qualifications to clarify our understanding of how God spoke His Word.

First, *God's Word* (now recorded in Scripture) *was closely related to His activity.* Put differently, He spoke to His people by deeds as well as words. He made Himself known to Israel in their history, and so directed its development as to bring to them now His salvation, now His judgment. Thus, He rescued the people from their slavery in Egypt; He brought them safely across the desert and settled them in the promised land; He preserved their national identity through the period of judges; He gave them kings to rule over them, despite the fact that their demand for a human king was in part a repudiation of His own kingship; His judgment fell upon them for their persistent disobedience when they were deported into Babylonian exile; and then He restored them to their own land and enabled them to rebuild their nationhood and their temple. Above all, for us sinners and for our salvation, He sent His eternal Son, Jesus Christ, to be born, to live and work, to suffer and die, to rise and to pour out the Holy Spirit. Through these deeds, first in the Old Testament story but supremely in Jesus Christ, God was actively and personally revealing Himself.

For this reason it has been fashionable for some theologians to distinguish sharply between "personal" revelation (through God's deeds) and "propositional" revelation (through His words), and then to reject the latter in favor of the former. This polarization, however, is as unfortunate as it is unnecessary. There is no need for us to choose between these two media of revelation. God used them both. Moreover, they were closely related to one another. For God's words interpreted His deeds. He raised up the prophets to explain what He was doing to Israel, and He raised up the apostles to explain what He was doing through Christ. It is true that the process of divine self-revelation culminated in the person of Jesus. He was God's Word made flesh. He showed forth the glory of God. To have seen Him was to have seen the Father (cf. John 1:14,18; 14:9). Nevertheless, this historical and personal revelation would not have benefited us unless, along with it, God had unfolded for us the significance of the person and work of His Son.

We must, then, avoid the trap of setting "personal" and "propositional" revelation over against each other as alternatives. It is more accurate to say that God has revealed Himself in Christ and in the biblical witness to Christ. Neither is complete without the other.

Second, *God's Word has come to us through human words.* When God spoke, He didn't shout to people out of a clear blue sky, audibly. No, He spoke *through* prophets (in the Old Testament) and *through* apostles (in the New Testament). Moreover, these human agents of the revelation of God were real people. Divine inspiration was not a *mechanical* process that reduced the human authors of the Bible to machines, whether dictating machines or tape recorders. Divine inspiration was a *personal* process, in which the human authors of the Bible were usually in full possession of their faculties. We have only to read the Bible to see that this is so. The writers of narrative (and there is a great deal of historical narrative in the Bible, Old and New Testament alike) used historical records. Some are quoted in the Old Testament. Luke tells us at the beginning of his gospel of his own painstaking historical researches. Next, all the biblical authors developed their own distinctive library styles and theological emphases. Hence the rich diversity of Scripture. Nevertheless, through their varied approaches God Himself was speaking.

This truth of the double authorship of the Bible (the Word of God and the word of men, or more strictly the Word of God through the words of men) is the Bible's own account of itself. The Old Testament law, for example, is sometimes called "the law of

Moses" and sometimes "the law of God" or "the law of the Lord." In Hebrews 1:1 we read that God spoke to the fathers through the prophets. In 2 Peter 1:21, however, we read that *men* spoke from God as they were moved by the Holy Spirit. Thus, God spoke and men spoke. They spoke "from" Him, and He spoke "through" them. Both of these affirmations are true.

Further, we must hold the two affirmations together. As in the incarnate Word (Jesus Christ), so in the written Word (the Bible) the divine and human elements combine and do not contradict one another. This analogy, which was developed quite early in the history of the church, is often criticized today. And obviously it is not exact, since Jesus was a person, whereas the Bible is a book. Nevertheless, the analogy remains helpful, provided that we remember its limitations. For example, we must never affirm the deity of Jesus in such a way as to deny His humanity, nor affirm His humanity in such a way as to deny His Deity. So with the Bible. On the one hand, the Bible is the Word of God. God spoke, deciding Himself what He intended to say, yet not in such a way as to distort the personality of the human authors. On the other hand, the Bible is the word of men. Men spoke, using their faculties freely, yet not in such a way as to distort the truth of the divine message.

The double authorship of the Bible will affect the way we read it. Because it is the word of men, we shall study it like every other book, using our minds, investigating its words and syntax, its historical origins and its literary compositions. But because it is also the Word of God, we shall study it like no other book, on our knees, humbly, crying to God for illumination and for the ministry of the Holy Spirit, without whom we can never understand His Word.

The purpose of revelation

We have considered how God spoke: Now, why did He speak? The answer is not just to teach us, but to save us; not just to instruct us, but specifically to instruct us "for salvation" (2 Tim. 3:15). The Bible has this severely practical purpose.

Returning to Isaiah 55, this is the emphasis of verses 10 and 11. The rain and the snow come down to us from heaven and do not return there. They accomplish a purpose on earth. They water it. They cause it to bring forth and sprout. They make it fruitful. Just so, God's Word, issuing from His mouth and disclosing His mind, does not return to Him empty. It accomplishes a purpose. Moreover, God's purpose in sending rain to the earth and His purpose in speaking His Word to human beings are similar. In both cases it is fruitfulness. His rain makes the earth fruitful; His Word makes human lives fruitful. It saves them, changing them into the likeness of Jesus Christ. Salvation is certainly the context. For in verse 7 the prophet has spoken of God's mercy and pardon, and in verse 12 he will go on to speak of the joy and peace of God's redeemed people.

In fact, here lies the chief difference between God's revelation in creation ("natural," because given in nature, and "general" because given to all mankind) and His revelation in the Bible ("supernatural," because given by inspiration, and "special," because given to and through particular people). Through the created universe God reveals His glory, power, and faithfulness, but not the way of salvation. If we want to learn His gracious plan to save sinners, it is to the Bible that we must turn. For it is there that He speaks to us of Christ.

Conclusion

From our text in Isaiah 55 we have learned three truths.

First, divine revelation is not only reasonable, but indispensable. Without it we could never know God.

Second, divine revelation is through words. God spoke through human words and in doing so was explaining His deeds.

Third, divine revelation is for salvation. It points us to Christ as Savior.

My conclusion is very simple. It is a call to humility. Nothing is more hostile to spiritual growth than arrogance, and nothing is more conducive to spiritual growth than humility. We need to humble ourselves before the infinite God, acknowledging the limitations of our human mind (that we could never find Him by ourselves), and acknowledging our own sinfulness (that we could never reach Him by ourselves).

Jesus called this the humility of a little child. God hides Himself from the "learned," He said, but reveals Himself to "little children" (Matt. 11:25). He was not denigrating our minds, for God has given them to us. Rather was He indicating how we are to use them. The true function of the mind is not to stand in judgment on God's Word, but to sit in humility under it, eager to hear it, grasp it, apply it, and obey it in the practicalities of daily living.

The "humility" of children is seen not only in the way they learn, but also in the way they receive. Children are dependants. None of their possessions has been earned. All they have has been given to them freely. Like children, then, we are to "receive the kingdom of God" (Mark 10:15). For sinners do not deserve, and cannot earn, eternal life (which is the life of God's kingdom); we have to humble ourselves to receive it as the free gift of God.

2. Christ and the Bible

Our first topic was "God and the Bible." We considered the origin of Scripture, where it came from—the great subject of revelation. Our second topic is "Christ and the Bible." We shall be thinking now not of its origin but of its purpose; not where has it come from, but what has it been given for?

Our text is John 5:39-40. Jesus is speaking to His Jewish contemporaries and says,

> *You diligently study the Scriptures because you think that by them you possess eternal life. These are the Scriptures that testify about me, yet you refuse to come to me to have life.*

From these words of Jesus we learn two profound and complementary truths about Christ and the Bible.

The Scriptures bear witness to Christ

Jesus Himself says so very plainly: "These are the Scriptures that testify about me" (v. 39). The major function of Scripture is to bear witness to Christ.

Now the context in which this text is embedded is concerned with testimony to Christ. What testimony can validate the claims of Jesus of Nazareth? He Himself tells us. To begin with, He does not rely on His own testimony to Himself, as is clear from verse 31: "If I testify about myself, my testimony is not valid." Of course Jesus is not suggesting that He is telling lies about Himself. Indeed, He later rebuts a criticism of the Pharisees by insisting that His testimony to Himself is true (8:14). His point here is that self-testimony is inadequate; there would be something suspicious about it if the only testimony He had came from Him alone. "There is another who testifies in my favor," He says (v. 32). So the testimony He relies upon is not His own testimony. Nor is it human testimony, even the testimony of that outstanding witness, John the Baptist. "You have sent to John and he has testified to the truth. Not that I accept human testimony . . ." (vv. 33-34). So then, it isn't from Me, and it isn't from human beings, says Jesus. Of course, John was "a lamp that burned and gave light" (v. 35), and they had been willing "for a time to enjoy his light." But the testimony that Jesus claimed was greater. It was greater than His own testimony to Himself, and greater than the testimony of any human being, even of John. It was the testimony of His Father. "The Father who sent me has Himself testified concerning me" (v. 37). Moreover, the Father's testimony to the Son took two forms. First, it was through the mighty works, the miracles, which the Father enabled Him to do (v. 36). But second, and more directly still, it was given through the Scriptures, which are the Father's testimony to the Son. Verses 36 through 39 make this plain.

> *I have testimony weightier than that of John. For the very work that the Father has given me to finish, and which I am doing, testifies that the Father has sent me. And the Father who sent me has himself testified concerning me. You have never heard his voice, nor seen his form, nor does his word dwell in you, for you do not believe the one he sent. You diligently study the Scriptures because you think that by them you possess eternal life. These are the Scriptures that testify about me.*

It was the consistent teaching of Jesus that Old Testament Scripture was God's Word bearing witness to Him. For example, He said, "Abraham rejoiced to see my day" (John 8:56, AV). Or here in John 5:46 He says, "Moses . . . wrote of me" (AV). Again, "The Scriptures . . . testify of me" (v. 39). At the beginning of His ministry, when He went to worship in the synagogue at Nazareth, you will remember, He read from Isaiah 61 about the Messiah's mission and message of liberation and added: "Today this scripture is fulfilled in your hearing" (Luke 4:21). In other words, "If you want to know whom the prophet was writing about, He was writing about Me." Jesus continued to say this kind of thing throughout His ministry. Even after the resurrection He had not changed His mind, for "he explained to them what was said in all the Scriptures concerning himself" (Luke 24:27). Thus from the beginning to the end of His ministry Jesus declared that the whole prophetic testimony of the Old Testament, in all its rich diversity, converged upon Him. "The Scriptures . . . testify about me."

But Jesus' Jewish contemporaries missed this testimony. They were untiring students of the Old Testament, and we have no quarrel with them over their study. "You diligently study the Scriptures," Jesus said. They did. They spent hours and hours in the most meticulous examination of the minutiae of Old Testament Scripture. They used to count the number of words, even the number of letters, in every book of the Bible. They knew they had been entrusted with the oracles of God (Rom. 3:2). They somehow thought that an accumulation of detailed biblical knowledge would bring them into right relationship with God. "You diligently study the Scriptures because you think that by them you possess eternal life." What an anomalous thing that was, to imagine that the Scriptures themselves could give eternal life! The Scriptures point to Christ as the Lifegiver and urge their readers to go to Him for life. But instead of going to Christ to find life, they imagined that they could find life in Scripture

Christ and the Bible

itself. It is somewhat like getting a prescription from the doctor and then swallowing the prescription instead of getting and taking the medicine!

Some of us make the same mistake. We have an almost superstitious attitude toward Bible reading, as if it had some magical efficacy. But there is no magic in the Bible or in the mechanical reading of the Bible. No, the written Word points to the Living Word and says to us, "Go to Jesus." If we do not go to the Jesus to whom it points, we miss the whole purpose of Bible reading. Evangelical Christians are not, or ought not to be, what we are sometimes accused of being, namely "bibliolaters," worshipers of the Bible. No, we do not worship the Bible; we worship the Christ of the Bible.

Here is a young man who is in love. He has a girlfriend who has captured his heart. Or indeed she may be his fiancée, or his wife, and he is deeply in love with her. As a result he carries a photograph of his beloved in his wallet, because it reminds him of her when she is far away. Sometimes, when nobody is looking, he might even take the photograph out and give it a surreptitious kiss. But kissing the photograph is a poor substitute for the real thing. And so it is with the Bible. We love it only because we love Him of whom it speaks.

That is the main key to the understanding of Scripture. The Bible is God's picture of Jesus. It bears witness to Him. So whenever we are reading the Bible, we must look for Christ. For example, the Old Testament law is our "schoolmaster" to bring us to

Christ (Gal. 3:24, AV). Because it condemns us for our disobedience, it makes Christ indispensable to us. It drives us to Him, through whom alone we may find forgiveness.

Next, the Old Testament sacrifices foreshadow that perfect sacrifice for sin made once for all upon the cross—the sacrifice of Christ for our redemption. Another example is the teaching of the Old Testament prophets who foretell the coming of the Messiah. They speak of Him as a king of David's line, during whose kingdom there will be peace, righteousness, and stability. They write of Him as "the seed of Abraham" through whom all nations of the world will be blessed. They depict Him as the "suffering servant of the Lord" who will die for the sins of His people, and as "the son of man coming in the clouds of heaven," whom all peoples will serve. All this rich imagery of Old Testament prophecy bears witness to Christ.

When we move into the New Testament, Jesus Christ comes yet more clearly into focus. The Gospels are full of Him. They speak of His birth and of His public ministry, of His words and works, of His death and resurrection, and of His ascension and gift of the Holy Spirit. The book of Acts tells us what Jesus continued to do and to teach through the apostles whom He had chosen and commissioned. The letters of the apostles set forth the glory of Jesus in His divine-human person and His saving work.

When you come to the last book of the Bible, the Revelation, it too is full of Christ. For there we see

Him patrolling the churches on earth, sharing God's throne in heaven, riding forth on a white horse conquering, and coming in glory and power.

The old writers used to say that just as in England every footpath and every country lane, linking on to others, will ultimately lead you to London, so every verse and every paragraph in the Bible, linking on to others, will ultimately lead you to Christ. The Scriptures bear witness to Him. That is the first truth that is very plainly taught in my text.

Christ bears witness to the Scriptures

In declaring that the Scriptures bear witness to Him, Jesus is Himself bearing witness to them. When He spoke of the testimony of John the Baptist, He referred to it as human testimony (John 5:33-34), and added that the testimony that attested Him was not human testimony. The testimony He had was greater. It was His Father's testimony through His works (v. 36) and His word (v. 38). Here, then, is Jesus' plain statement that the Old Testament Scriptures are His Father's "word," and that this biblical testimony was not human, but divine.

This too was Jesus' consistent teaching. In fact, the major reason why we desire to submit to the authority of the Bible is that Jesus Christ authenticated it as possessing the authority of God. If we are to understand this point (as understand it we must), then we need to distinguish between the Old and the New Testaments. The Bible, of course, comprises them

31

both, but Jesus was born and lived and died in the middle, between them. As a consequence, the way in which He authenticated the one is different from the way in which He authenticated the other. He looked back to the Old Testament, He looked on to the New Testament, but He authenticated them both.

a. Jesus endorsed the Old Testament

He not only described it as His Father's "word" and "witness," as we have seen, He also said, "Scripture cannot be broken" (John 10:35). At the beginning of the Sermon on the Mount, He declared: "Do not think that I have come to abolish the Law or the Prophets; I have not come to abolish them but to fulfill them. I tell you the truth, until heaven and earth disappear, not the smallest letter, not the least stroke of a pen, will by any means disappear from the Law until everything is accomplished" (Matt. 5:17-18). His personal attitude toward the Old Testament Scriptures was one of reverent submission, for He believed that in submitting to the written Word, He was submitting to His Father's Word. Since He believed in its divine origin, He interpreted His own messianic mission in the light of its prophetic testimony and added that certain things must come to pass, because Scripture must be fulfilled.

Further, Jesus obeyed the moral injunctions of the Old Testament, as when in the temptations in the Judean wilderness He commanded the devil to leave Him because of what stood written in Scripture. However subtle Satan's insinuations might be, Jesus was prepared neither to listen nor to negotiate. He was determined to obey God, not the devil, and what stood written in Scripture settled the issue for Him (e.g., Luke 4:4, 8, 12).

Jesus also made the Scripture His ground of appeal in all His arguments with the religious leaders of His day. He was often engaged in controversy, and on every occasion it was to the Scriptures that He appealed. He criticized the Pharisees for adding their traditions to the Scriptures, and the Sadducees for subtracting the supernatural (e.g., the resurrection) from the Scriptures. Thus Jesus exalted Scripture as His Father's Word, to be both believed and obeyed. He permitted no deviation from it, either by addition or by subtraction.

Of course He declared that, with Him, the time of "fulfillment" had come (e.g., Mark 1:14-15), and that therefore the era of anticipation was over. This meant, as His followers soon recognized, that Gentiles were to be admitted to God's kingdom on equal terms with Jews, and that the Jewish ceremonial system had been rendered obsolete, including its dietary laws (Mark 7:19) and above all its blood sacrifices. But there is no example in the Gospels of Jesus disagreeing with the doctrinal or ethical teaching of the Old Testament. What He contradicted was the scribal misinterpretations and distortions of the Old Testament. This was His point in the Sermon on the Mount, in which six times He said in effect, "You have heard this, but I tell you something different." What they had "heard" was the so-called "traditions of the elders." It was these that

He was criticizing; it was not the teaching of Moses in the law. For what stood written in Scripture He received as His Father's Word.

If this is so, and the evidence is overwhelming, we have to add that the disciple is not above his teacher. It is inconceivable that a Christian who looks to Jesus as his Teacher and Lord should have a lower view of the Old Testament than He had. What is the sense in calling Jesus "Teacher" and "Lord," and then disagreeing with Him? We have no liberty to disagree with Him. His view of Scripture must become ours. Since He believed Scripture, so must we. Since He obeyed Scripture, so must we. He emphatically endorsed its authority.

b. *Jesus made provision for the writing of the New Testament.*

Just as God called the prophets in the Old Testament to record and interpret what He was doing and then "sent" them to teach the children of Israel, so Jesus called the apostles to record and interpret what He was doing and saying and then "sent" them to teach the church, and indeed the world. This is the meaning of the word *apostolos*, a person sent on a mission with a message. This parallel between the Old Testament prophets and the New Testament apostles was deliberate. Jesus chose twelve in order that they might be with Him—to hear His words, see His works, and then bear witness out of what they had seen and heard (cf. Mark 3:14; John 15:27). Next, He promised them the Holy Spirit to remind them of His teaching and to supplement it, leading them into all the truth (John 14:25-26; 16:12-13). This explains why Jesus could then say to the apostles, "He who listens to you listens to Me; he who receives you receives me; he who rejects you rejects me" (see Matt. 10:40; Luke 10:16; John 13:20). In other words, He invested them with His authority, so that people's attitude toward their teaching would mirror their attitude toward His. Later Jesus added Paul and maybe one or two others to the apostolic band, investing them with the same apostolic authority.

The apostles themselves recognized the unique authority they had been given as the teachers of the church. They did not hesitate on occasions to put themselves on a par with the Old Testament prophets, since they too were bearers of "the word of God" (e.g., 1 Thess. 2:13). They spoke and wrote in the name and with the authority of Jesus Christ. They issued commandments and expected obedience (e.g., 2 Thess. 3). They even gave instructions that their letters should be read in the public assembly when Christians were gathered together for worship, thus placing them alongside the Old Testament Scriptures (e.g., Col. 4:16; 1 Thess. 5:27). This is the origin of the practice, which continues to this day, of having an Old Testament and a New Testament lesson read in church.

A striking example of Paul's self-conscious apostolic authority occurs in his letter to the Galatians. He had climbed over the Taurus mountains on to the Galatian plateau to visit them and had arrived a sick man. He mentions some disfigurement, which had perhaps affected his eyesight (4:13), and goes on to say: "You did not treat me with contempt or scorn. Instead, you welcomed me as if I were an angel of God, as if I were Christ Jesus himself" (v. 14). Notice that he does not rebuke them for this. He doesn't say, "What on earth were you thinking about, that you should have given to me the deference that you would give to Christ?" No, he applauds them for the way they had treated him. It was not merely Christian courtesy which had motivated them to welcome a stranger. It was more than that. They had recognized him as a divine messenger, an apostle, who had come to them in the name and with the authority of Christ. So they had received him as if he were Christ.

Not only did the apostles understand the teaching authority they had been given, but the early church understood it also. As soon as all the apostles had died, church leaders knew that they had moved into a new post-apostolic era. There was now no longer anybody in the church with the authority of a Paul or a Peter or a John. Bishop Ignatius of Antioch is perhaps the earliest clear example of this, about A.D. 110, which was very soon after John, the last surviving apostle, had died. On his way to Rome to be executed, Ignatius wrote a number of letters to the Ephesians, the Romans, the Trallians, and others. Several times in these he wrote: "I do not, like Peter or Paul, issue you with commands. For I am not an apostle, but a condemned man." Now Ignatius was a bishop in the church. He is, in fact, one of the earliest witnesses to the rise of the episcopate.

But, although he was a bishop, he knew he was not an apostle, and he therefore did not have an apostle's authority.

The early church clearly understood this difference. When the time came to fix the New Testament canon in the third century A.D., the test of canonicity was apostolicity. The essential questions to be asked of a disputed book were these: Had it been written by an apostle? If not, did it come from the circle of the apostles? Did it contain the teaching of the apostles? Did it have the imprimatur of the apostles? If in one of these ways it could be shown to be "apostolic," then its place in the canon of New Testament Scripture was secure.

It is extremely important to recover today this understanding of the unique authority of Christ's apostles. For there are no apostles in the contemporary church. To be sure, there are missionaries and church leaders of different kinds who may be described as having an "apostolic" ministry, but there are no apostles like the Twelve and Paul who were eyewitnesses of the risen Lord (Acts 1:21-26; 1 Cor. 9:1; 15:8-10), and who had received a special commission and inspiration from him. We have no right, therefore, to dismiss their teaching as if it were merely their own opinions. They were not speaking or writing in their own name, but in Christ's.

Conclusion
Let me sum up. We believe the Scriptures because of

Christ. He endorsed the Old Testament and He made provision for the writing of the New Testament by giving to the apostles His authority. We therefore receive the Bible from the hand of Jesus Christ. It is He who has invested it with His own authority. And since we are determined to submit to Him, we are determined to submit to it. Our doctrine of Scripture is bound up with our loyalty to Jesus Christ. If He is our Teacher and our Lord, we have no liberty to disagree with Him. Our view of Scripture must be His.

At this point some people raise an understandable objection. "The Scriptures bear witness to Christ and Christ bears witness to the Scriptures," they say, accurately summarizing what we have been saying. "But surely," they continue, "this reciprocal testimony, each bearing witness to the other, is a circular argument? Does it not assume the very truth you are wanting to prove? That is, to demonstrate the inspiration of Scripture, you appeal to the teaching of Jesus, but you believe the teaching of Jesus only because of the inspired Scriptures. Isn't that a circular argument, and therefore invalid?" Well, this is an important objection to face. But actually our argument has been misstated, for it is linear and not circular reasoning.

Let me put it this way: When we first listen to the biblical witness to Christ, we read our New Testament with no preconceived doctrine of inspiration. We simply accept it as a collection of first-century historical documents, which indeed it is. Through this historical testimony, however, quite apart from any theory of biblical inspiration, the Holy Spirit brings us to faith in Jesus. Then this Jesus, in whom we have come to believe, sends us back to the Bible and gives us in His teaching a doctrine of Scripture that we did not have when we started our reading. For He now tells us that its *historical* testimony is also *divine* testimony, and that through the human agency of prophets and apostles His Father is bearing witness to Him.

Whenever you read the Bible, I want to beg you to remember its major purpose. Scripture is the Father's testimony to the Son. It points to Him. It says to us, "Go to Him in order to find life—abundant life—in Him." Therefore any preoccupation with the biblical text that does not lead to a stronger commitment to Jesus Christ, in faith, love, worship, and obedience, is seriously perverted. It brings us under the rebuke of Jesus. "You diligently study the Scriptures because you think that by them you possess eternal life. These are the Scriptures that testify about me, yet you refuse to come to me [to whom they testify] to have life."

Scripture (as Luther used to say) is the manger or "cradle" in which the infant Jesus lies. Don't let us inspect the cradle and forget to worship the Baby. Scripture, we might say, is the star that still leads wise people to Jesus. Don't let us allow our astronomical curiosity to so preoccupy us that we miss the house to which it is leading, and within it the Christ-child Himself. Again, we might say, Scripture is the box in which the jewel of Jesus Christ is displayed. Don't let us admire the box and overlook the jewel.

Dr. Christopher Chavasse, formerly Bishop of Rochester, once put the matter admirably when he said:

> The Bible is the portrait of our Lord Jesus Christ. The Gospels are the Figure itself in the portrait. The Old Testament is the background leading up to the divine Figure, pointing towards it and absolutely necessary to the composition as a whole. The Epistles serve as the dress and accoutrements of the Figure, explaining and describing it. Then while by our Bible reading we study the portrait as a great whole, the miracle happens, the Figure comes to life, and stepping down from the canvas of the written word the everlasting Christ of the Emmaus story becomes Himself our Bible teacher, to interpret to us in all the Scriptures the things concerning Himself.

You see, it is not enough to possess a Bible, to read the Bible, love the Bible, study the Bible, know the Bible. We need to ask ourselves: Is the Christ of the Bible the center of our lives? If not, all our Bible reading has been futile, for this is the end to which the Bible is intended to be the means.

3. The Holy Spirit and the Bible

All Christians know that the Holy Bible and the Holy Spirit are supposed to have something to do with each other. Indeed, all Christians believe that in some sense the Holy Bible is the creative product of the Holy Spirit. For whenever we say the Nicene Creed, we affirm as one of our beliefs about the Holy Spirit that "He spoke through the prophets." This expression echoes many similar phrases which occur in the New Testament. For example, our Lord Jesus Himself once introduced a quotation from Psalm 110 with the words: "David himself, speaking by the Holy Spirit, declared . . ." (Mark 12:36). Similarly, the apostle Peter in his second letter wrote that "men spoke from God as they were carried along by the Holy Spirit" (2 Peter 1:21); they were "carried along" by the Holy Spirit as if by a powerful wind. There is then an important relationship between the Bible and the Spirit that we need to investigate.

So far we have considered that God is the author of the revelation that has been given, and that Jesus Christ is its principal subject. Now we have to add that the Holy Spirit is its agent. Thus the Christian understanding of the Bible is essentially a Trinitarian understanding. The Bible comes from God, centers on Christ, and is inspired by the Holy Spirit. So the best definition of the Bible is also Trinitarian: The Bible is the witness of the Father to the Son through the Holy Spirit.

What, then, is the precise role of the Holy Spirit in the process of revelation? To answer this question we turn to the Bible itself and in particular to 1 Corinthians 2:6-16.

> We do, however, speak a message of wisdom among the mature, but not the wisdom of this age or of the rulers of this age, who are coming to nothing. No, we speak of God's secret wisdom, a wisdom that has been hidden and that God destined for our glory before time began. None of the rulers of this age understood it, for if they had, they would not have crucified the Lord of glory. However, as it is written,
> "No eye has seen,
> no ear heard,
> no mind has conceived
> what God has prepared for those who love
> him"—
> but God has revealed it to us by his Spirit.

The Holy Spirit and the Bible

The Spirit searches all things, even the deep things of God. For who among men knows the thoughts of a man except the man's spirit within him? In the same way no one knows the thoughts of God except the Spirit of God. We have not received the spirit of the world but the Spirit who is from God, that we may understand what God has freely given us. This is what we speak, not in words taught us by human wisdom but in words taught by the Spirit, expressing spiritual truths in spiritual words. The man without the Spirit does not accept the things that come from the Spirit of God, for they are foolishness to him, and he cannot understand them, because they are spiritually discerned. The spiritual man makes judgments about all things, but he himself is not subject to any man's judgment:

> *"For who has known the mind of the Lord*
> *that he may instruct him?"*

But we have the mind of Christ.

It is important that we see this text in its wider context. Up to this point in 1 Corinthians, Paul has been emphasizing the "foolishness" of the gospel. For example, "the message of the cross is *foolishness* to those who are perishing" (1:18), and "we preach Christ crucified: a stumbling block to Jews and *foolishness* to Gentiles" (1:23). Or, as we might put it today, the message of the cross sounds stupid to secular intellectuals, even meaningless. So Paul now adds a corrective, lest his readers should imagine that he is repudiating wisdom altogether, and that he glories in folly instead. Is the apostle anti-intellectual, then? Does he scorn understanding and the use of the mind? No, indeed not.

"We do, however, speak a message of wisdom among the mature, . . . a wisdom that has been hidden and that God destined for our glory" (2:6-7). The contrasts that Paul is making must not be overlooked. We do impart wisdom, he writes, but (a) only to the mature, not to non-Christians or even to very young Christians; (b) it is God's wisdom, not worldly wisdom; and (c) it is for our *glory*, that is, our final perfection through sharing in God's glory, and not just to bring us to justification in Christ. We ourselves need to follow the apostle's example. In evangelizing non-Christians we must concentrate on the "foolishness" of the gospel of Christ crucified for sinners. In building up Christians into full maturity, however, we should want to lead them into an understanding of God's total purpose. Paul calls this in verse 7 God's "secret" wisdom and in verse 9, "what God has prepared for those who love him." It can be known, he stresses, only by revelation. "The rulers of this age" (secular leaders) did not understand it, or they would never have crucified "the Lord of glory" (v. 8). They were not exceptional, however; all human beings, if left to themselves, are ignorant of God's wisdom and purpose.

For God's purpose, Paul writes here (v. 9) is something which "no eye has seen" (it is invisible), "no ear has heard" (it is inaudible), "no mind has conceived" (it is inconceivable). It is beyond the reach of human eyes, ears, and minds. It is not amenable to scientific investigation, nor even to poetic imagination. It is altogether beyond our little finite minds to fathom, unless God should reveal it. Which is exactly what God has done! Listen again: "No eye has seen, no ear has heard, no mind has conceived what God has prepared for those who love him"—this unimaginable splendor of His purpose—"but God has revealed it to us by his Spirit." The word "us" is emphatic, and in the context must refer not to all of us indiscriminately, but to the apostle Paul who is writing, and to his fellow apostles. God gave a special revelation of these truths to special organs of revelation (the prophets in the Old Testament and the apostles in the New), and God did this "by his Spirit." The Holy Spirit has been the agent of this revelation.

All of this is, I'm afraid, a rather lengthy introduction to help us see the context within which Paul comes to his theme of the Holy Spirit as the agent of revelation. What he goes on to write is a marvelously comprehensive statement. He outlines the four stages of the Holy Spirit's work as agent of divine revelation.

The searching Spirit
First, the Holy Spirit is the searching Spirit (vv. 10-11).

It is worth noting, just in passing, that this shows the Holy Spirit to be personal. Only persons can engage in "search" or "research." To be sure, modern computers can undertake highly complex research of a mechanical, analytical kind. But true research (as all postgraduate research students know well) involves more than the compilation and analysis of statistical data; it requires original thought, both in investigation and in reflection. This, then, is work that the Holy Spirit does, because He has a mind with which He thinks. Being a Divine person (and not a computer, or a vague influence or power), we need to accustom ourselves to referring to the Spirit as "He" not "It."

Paul uses two fascinating little pictures to indicate the unique qualifications of the Holy Spirit in the work of revelation.

The first is that "the Spirit searches all things, even the deep things of God" (v. 10). It is the same verb that Jesus applied to the Jews who "diligently study the Scriptures" (John 5:39). The Holy Spirit is depicted as a restlessly inquisitive research worker, or even (though "the deep things of God" was a favorite expression of Gnostic heretics, and Paul may be borrowing it from their vocabulary) as a deep-sea diver who is seeking to fathom the deepest parts of the Being of Almighty God. For God's Being is infinite in its profundity, and Paul boldly declares the the Spirit of God is searching the depths of God. In other words, God Himself is exploring the riches of His own Being.

The Holy Spirit and the Bible

The second model or picture Paul gives is taken from human self-understanding. "For who among men knows the thoughts of a man except the man's spirit within him?" (v. 11). "Thoughts" is literally "things," a human being's "things," perhaps what we would call our "humanness." An ant cannot possibly conceive what it is like to be a human being. Nor can a frog, or a rabbit, or even the most intelligent ape. Nor can one human being fully understand another human being. How often we say, particularly in adolescence, "You just don't understand; nobody understands me." That is true! Nobody does understand me except myself, and even my understanding of myself is limited. In the same way nobody understands you except yourself. This measure of self-understanding or self-consciousness Paul applies to the Holy Spirit: "In the same way no one knows the thoughts of God except the Spirit of God" (v. 11). The Holy Spirit of God is here almost likened to the divine self-understanding or the divine self-consciousness. Just as nobody can understand a human being except that human being himself, so nobody can understand God except God Himself. We sometimes sing in a hymn, "God only knows the love of God." We could equally well affirm that only God knows the wisdom of God, indeed only God knows the Being of God.

So, then, the Spirit searches the depths of God, and the Spirit knows the things of God. He has an understanding of God that is unique. The question now is: What has He done with what He has searched out and come to know? Has He kept His unique knowledge to Himself? No. He has done what only He is competent to do; He has revealed it. The searching Spirit has become the revealing Spirit.

The revealing Spirit

What the Holy Spirit alone has come to know, He alone has made known. This has already been stated in verse 10: "God has revealed it to us [the apostles] by his Spirit." Now Paul elaborates upon this in verse 12: "We" (the same apostolic "we," the plural of apostolic authority) "have not received the spirit of the world but the Spirit who is from God" (namely the searching and knowing Spirit), "that we may understand what God has freely given us." The apostles had, in fact, received two gracious gifts from God: the first His grace in salvation ("what God has freely given us"), and the second His Spirit to enable them to understand His gracious salvation.

Paul himself is the best example of this double process. As we read his letters, he gives us a superb exposition of the gospel of God's grace. He tells us what God has done for guilty sinners like us who are without excuse and deserve nothing at His hand but judgment. He declares that God sent His Son to die for our sins on the cross and rise again, and that if we are united to Jesus Christ, by faith inwardly and by baptism outwardly, then we die with Him and rise again with Him and experience a new life in Him. It is a magnificent gospel that Paul unfolds in his letters. But how does he know all this? How can he make such comprehensive statements of salvation? First, because he has himself received it. He knows the grace of God in experience. Second, the Holy Spirit has been given to him to interpret his own experience to him. Thus the Holy Spirit revealed to him God's plan of salvation, what Paul calls "the mystery" in other epistles. The searching Spirit became the revealing Spirit.

The inspiring Spirit

Now we are ready for stage three: the revealing Spirit became the inspiring Spirit. "This is what we speak, not in words taught us by human wisdom but in words taught by the Spirit" (v. 13). Notice that in verse 12 Paul writes of what we have received, and in verse 13 of what we impart. I might elaborate his sequence of thought like this: "We have received these gracious gifts of God; we have received this Spirit to interpret to us what God has done for us and given to us; now, we impart to others what we have received." The searching Spirit, who had revealed God's plan of salvation to the apostles, went on to communicate this gospel through the apostles to others. Just as the Spirit did not keep His reaches to Himself, so the apostles did not keep His revelation to themselves. No. They understood that they were trustees of it. They had to deliver to others what they had received.

Moreover, what they imparted was in words, and their words are specifically described as not "words taught us by human wisdom but in words taught by the Spirit" (v. 13). See how the Holy Spirit is mentioned again, this time as the inspiring Spirit? For here in verse 13 is an ambiguous claim on the part of the apostle Paul to "verbal inspiration." That is to say, the very words with which the apostles clothe the message that had been revealed to them by the Spirit were words taught them by the same Spirit.

I strongly suspect that the reason why the notion of "verbal inspiration" is unpopular today is that people misunderstand it. In consequence, what they are rejecting is not its true meaning, but a caricature. So let me try to clear the concept of some major misconceptions. First, "verbal inspiration" does not mean that "every word of the Bible is literally true." No, we fully recognize that the biblical authors used many different literary genres, each of which must be interpreted according to its own rules — history as history, poetry as poetry, parable as parable, etc. What is inspired is the natural sense of the words, according to the author's intention, whether this is literal or figurative.

Second, "verbal inspiration" does not mean verbal dictation. Muslims believe that Allah dictated the Koran to Muhammad, word by word, in Arabic. Christians do not believe that about the Bible, for, as we have already seen and I shall further emphasize later, the Holy Spirit treated the biblical authors as persons, not machines. With a few minor exceptions they seem to have been in full possession of their faculties while the Spirit was communicating His Word through their words.

Third, "verbal inspiration" does not mean that every sentence of the Bible is God's Word, even in isolation from its context. For not everything contained in the Bible is affirmed by the Bible. A good example is the long speeches of Job's so-called "comforters." Their major thesis, repeated ad nauseam, namely that God was punishing Job for his personal sins, was mistaken. In the last chapter God says to them twice, "you have not spoken of me what is right" (42:7-8). So their words cannot be taken as God's words. They are included in order to be contradicted, not endorsed. The inspired Word of God is what is being affirmed, whether as instruction, command, or promise.

"Verbal inspiration" means that what the Holy Spirit has spoken and still speaks through the human authors, understood according to the plain, natural meaning of the words used, is true and without error. There is no need at all to be embarrassed by this Christian belief, or to be ashamed or afraid of it. On the contrary, it is eminently reasonable, because words are the units of which sentences are made up. Words are the building-blocks of speech. It is therefore impossible to frame a precise message without constructing precise sentences composed of precise words.

Think of the trouble we all take to compose a cable or telegram. Let us say we've got only twelve words. All the same, we are determined to send a message that will not only be understood, but that will not be misunderstood. So we draft it, redraft it, and draft it again. We scratch out a word here and we add a word there until we have polished our message to our satisfaction. Words matter. Every speaker who wants to communicate a message that will be understood and not misunderstood knows the importance of words. Every preacher who takes pains to prepare his sermons chooses his words with care. Every writer, whether of letters or articles or books, knows that words matter. Listen to what Charles Kingsley said in the middle of the last century: "These glorious things—words—are man's right alone. . . . Without words we should know no more of each other's hearts and thoughts than the dog knows of his fellow dog . . . for, if you will consider, you always think to yourself in words, though you do not speak them aloud; and without them all our thoughts would be mere blind longings, feelings which we could not understand ourselves." So we have to clothe our thoughts in words.

This, then, is the apostolic claim, that the same Holy Spirit of God, who searched the deep things of God and revealed His findings to the apostles, went on to communicate them through the apostles in words with which He Himself supplied them. He spoke His words through their words so that they were equally the words of God and the words of men. This is the double authorship of Scripture. It is also the meaning of "inspiration." The inspiration of Scripture was not a mechanical process. It was intensely personal, for it involved a Person (the Holy Spirit) speaking through persons (prophets and apostles) in such a way that His words were theirs, and their words were His, simultaneously.

The enlightening Spirit

We now come to the fourth stage in the Holy Spirit's work as the agent of revelation, and in this I shall describe Him as the "enlightening" Spirit. Let me set the scene.

How are we to think about the people who heard the apostles preaching and later read their letters? Were they left to fend for themselves? Were they obliged to struggle as best they could to understand the apostolic message? No. The same Spirit who was active in those who wrote the apostolic letters was also active in those who read them. Thus the Holy Spirit was working at both ends, as it were, inspiring the apostles and enlightening their hearers. This is already implied at the end of verse 13, a complicated phrase, which has been variously interpreted. I take the Revised Standard Version translation as correct, namely that the Holy Spirit was "interpreting spiritual truths to those who possess the Spirit." Possession of the Spirit was not limited to the biblical authors. Certainly His word of inspiration in them was unique; yet to it He added His work of interpretation.

Verses 14 and 15 elaborate this truth, and are in stark contrast to each other. Verse 14 begins by referring to "the man without the Spirit" (or "the natural man," AV), that is, the unregenerate person who is not a Christian. Verse 15, however, begins with a reference to "the spiritual man," the possessor of the Holy Spirit. Paul thus divides mankind into two clear-cut categories: "the natural" and "the spiritual," that is, those who possess natural, animal, or physical life, on the one hand, and on the other, those who have received spiritual or eternal life. The first category lack the Holy Spirit because they have never been born again, but the Holy Spirit dwells in those to whom He has given a new birth. The indwelling of the Holy Spirit, is, in fact, the distinguishing mark of the true Christian man and woman (Rom. 8:9).

What difference does it make whether we have the Holy Spirit or not? All the difference in the world!—especially to our understanding of spiritual truth. The unspiritual or unregenerate person, who has not received the Holy Spirit, doesn't receive the Holy Spirit, nor does he receive the things of the Spirit, because they are foolishness to him (v. 14). Not only does he fail to understand them, he is not even able to do so because they are "spiritually discerned." The spiritual person, on the other hand, the born-again Christian in whom the Holy Spirit dwells, "discerns" (it is the same Greek verb as in verse 14) "all things." Not, of course, that he becomes omniscient like God, but that all those things to which he was previously blind, and that God has revealed in Holy Scripture, begin to make sense to him. He understands what he had never understood before, even though he himself is not really understood. Literally, he "is discerned by no one." He remains an enigma, for he has an inner secret of spiritual life and truth that doesn't make sense to non-believers. This is hardly surprising, however, for nobody knows the mind of the Lord, or can instruct Him. And since they cannot understand Christ's mind, they cannot understand ours either, though we whom the Holy Spirit enlightens can dare to say, "we have the mind of Christ" (v. 16)—a truly amazing affirmation.

Is this your experience? Has the Bible become a new book to you? William Grimshaw, one of the great eighteenth-century evangelical leaders, told a friend after his conversion that "if God had drawn up his Bible to heaven, and sent him down another, it could not have been newer to him." It was a different book. I could say the same myself. I read the Bible daily before I was converted, because my mother brought me up to do so, but it was double-Dutch to me. I hadn't the foggiest idea what it was all about. But when I was born again and the Holy Spirit came to dwell within me, the Bible immediately began to be a new book to me. Of course I am not claiming that I understood everything. I am far from understanding everything today. But I began to understand things I had never understood before. What a marvelous experience this is! Don't think of the Bible as just a collection of musty old documents whose real place is in the library. Don't think of the pages of Scripture as if they are fossils whose real place is behind glass in a museum. No, God speaks through what He has spoken. Through the ancient text of Scripture the Holy Spirit can communicate with us today freshly, personally, and powerfully. "He who has an ear, let him hear what the Spirit says" ("is saying"—it is a present tense—through the Scriptures) "to the churches" (Rev. 2:7).

If the Holy Spirit speaks to us through the Scriptures today, you may be asking, why don't we all agree about everything? If the Spirit is the interpreter as well as the agent of God's revelation, why does He not lead us to a common mind? My answer to these questions may surprise you. It is that He does in fact enable us to agree much more than we disagree, and that we would agree with one another even more if we fulfilled the following four conditions.

First, we must accept the supreme authority of Scripture, and earnestly desire to submit to it. Among those who do so, a substantial Christian consensus already exists. The big and painful differences that remain, for example between the Roman Catholic Church and the Protestant Churches, are mainly attributable to the former's continuing unwillingness to declare that Scripture has supreme authority even over church traditions. Rome's official position (modified but not effectively altered by the Second Vatican Council) is still that "both Sacred Tradition and Sacred Scripture are to be accepted and venerated with the same sense of devotion and reverence." Now Protestants do not deny the importance of tradition, and some of us should have more respect for it, since the Holy Spirit has taught past generations of Christians and did not begin His instruction only with us! Nevertheless, when Scripture and tradition are in collision, we must allow Scripture to reform tradition, just as Jesus insisted with the "traditions of men" (cf. Mark 7:1-13). If the Church of Rome were to have the courage to renounce unbiblical traditions (e.g., its dogmas about the immaculate conception and bodily assumption of the Virgin Mary), immediately progress would be made towards agreement under the Word of God.

Second, we must remember that, as we have seen, the overriding purpose of Scripture is to bear witness to Christ as the all-sufficient Savior of sinners. When the sixteenth-century Reformers insisted on the "perspicuity" (i.e., clarity) of Scripture, and translated the Bible into the vernacular so that ordinary people could read it for themselves, they were referring to the way of salvation. They did not deny that the Scriptures contain "some things that are hard to understand" (as Peter said of Paul's letters, 2 Peter 3:16); what they were at pains to affirm was that the essential truths of salvation were plain for all to understand.

Third, we must apply sound principles of interpretation. It is of course perfectly possible to twist the Bible into meaning anything we like. But our business is Scripture interpreting, not Scripture twisting. Above all, we have to seek both the *original* sense according to the biblical author's intention, and the *natural* sense, which may be either literal or figurative, again according to the author's intention. These are respectively the principles of history and of simplicity. When they are applied with integrity and rigor, then the Bible controls us and not we it. In consequence, the area of Christian agreement increases.

Fourth, we must come to the biblical text with a recognition of our cultural prejudices and with a willingness to have them challenged and changed. If we come to Scripture with the proud presupposition that all our inherited beliefs and practices are correct, then of course we shall find in the Bible only what we want to find, namely the comfortable confirmation of the status quo. As a result, we shall also find ourselves in sharp disagreement with people who come to Scripture from different backgrounds and with different convictions, and find these confirmed. There is probably no commoner source of discord than this. It is only when we are brave and humble enough to allow the Spirit of God through the Word of God radically to call in question our most cherished opinions, that we are likely to find fresh unity through fresh understanding.

The "spiritual discernment" that the Holy Spirit promises is not given in defiance of these four commonplace conditions; it presupposes that they are accepted and fulfilled.

Conclusion

We have considered the Holy Spirit in four roles, as the searching Spirit, the revealing Spirit, the inspiring Spirit, and the enlightening Spirit. These are the four stages of His teaching ministry. First, He searches the depths of God and knows the thoughts of God. Second, He revealed His findings to the apostles. Third, He communicated *through* the apostles what He had revealed *to* them, and did so in words that He Himself supplied. Fourth, He enlightened the minds of the hearers, so that they could discern what He had revealed to and through the apostles, and He continues this work of illumination today in those who are willing to receive it.

There are two very simple and short lessons in closing. The first concerns our view of the Holy Spirit. Much is said today about the person and work of the Spirit, and this is only one of many passages in the Bible about Him. But let me ask you this: Is there room in your doctrine of the Spirit for this passage? Jesus called Him "the Spirit of truth." So truth is very important to the Holy Spirit. Oh, I know, He is also the Spirit of holiness, and the Spirit of love, and the Spirit of power, but is He to you the Spirit of *truth*? According to the verses we have been studying, He is deeply concerned about the truth. He searches it, has revealed and communicated it, and enlightens our minds to grasp it. Dear friend, never denigrate truth! Never disdain theology! Never despise your mind! If you do, you grieve the Holy Spirit of truth. This passage should affect our view of the Holy Spirit.

The second concern is our need of the Holy Spirit. Do you want to grow in your knowledge of God? Of course you do. Do you want to grow in your understanding of the wisdom of God and of the totality of His purpose to make us one day like Christ in glory? Of course you do. So do I. Then we need the Holy Spirit, the Spirit of truth, to illumine our minds. For that we need to be born again. I sometimes wonder if the reason why some secular theologians today are speaking and writing, if I may say so, such rubbish (I am referring for example, to their denial of personality to God and of deity to Jesus) is that they have never been born again. It is possible to be a theologian and unregenerate. Is that why they do not discern these marvelous truths of Scripture? Scripture is spiritually discerned. So we need to come to the Scriptures humbly, reverently, and expectantly. We need to acknowledge that the truths revealed in the Bible are still locked and sealed until the Holy Spirit opens them to us and opens our minds to them. For God hides them from the wise and clever and reveals them only to "children," those who are humble and reverent in their approach to Him. So then, before we preachers prepare, before a congregation listens, before an individual or a group begins to read the Bible—in these situations we must pray for the Holy Spirit's illumination. "Open my eyes that I may see wonderful things in your law" (Ps. 119:18). And He will.

4. The Church and the Bible

So far we have engaged in a Trinitarian study. We have seen that God is the author, Christ both the principal subject and the authenticating witness, and the Holy Spirit the agent of the great process of revelation. We come now to the church.

What do you think of the church? Your answer will probably depend on whether you are thinking about the ideal or the reality. In the ideal, the church is the most marvelous new creation of God. It is the new community of Jesus, enjoying a multi-racial, multi-national, and multi-cultural harmony that is unique in history and in contemporary society. The church is even the "new humanity," the vanguard of a redeemed and renewed human race. It is a people who spend their earthly lives (as they will also spend eternity) in the loving service of God and of others. What a noble and beautiful ideal! In reality, however, the church is us—a disheveled rabble of sinful, fallible, bickering, squabbling, stupid, shallow Christians, who constantly fall short of God's ideal, and often fail even to approximate to it.

Now, what is the reason for this gulf between the ideal and the reality? Why is the church in such a perilous condition throughout the world today— weak, fragmented, and making so little impact upon the world for Christ? I'm sure there are many reasons, but I believe the overwhelming reason is what Amos called "a famine . . . of hearing the words of the LORD" (Amos 8:11, AV), or in plain modern language, a neglect of the Bible. The multiple unfaithfulness of the church is due to its overriding unfaithfulness to the self-revelation of God in Scripture. The late Dr. Martyn Lloyd-Jones was right when he wrote in his book *Preaching and Preachers,* "The decadent eras and periods of the Church's history have always been those in which preaching has declined." In other words, the church remains sick and feeble whenever it refuses the healing medicine and wholesome nourishment of the Word of God.

We are now going to consider two texts, both of which use an architectural metaphor.

In Ephesians 2:20 the church, which has just been defined as God's "household" or family (v. 19) is further described as "built on the foundation of the apostles and prophets, with Christ Jesus himself as the chief cornerstone." That is, the teaching of the biblical authors is the foundation on which the church is built, as Jesus Christ is the cornerstone that holds it together.

In 1 Timothy 3:15 the metaphor is reversed. Having again referred to the church as "God's household," Paul now goes on to call it "the pillar and foundation of the truth."

You will observe that in the first text the truth is the foundation, and the church is the building it supports, while in the second text, the church is the foundation and the truth is the building that it supports.

"Well, there you are," I hear someone saying. "I told you so. The Bible is full of contradictions." Really? Wait a moment. Both these verses come from the pen of the same man, the apostle Paul. Let us give him credit for a little logical consistency. It has always been dangerous to use metaphors and similes. We have to inquire at what point the analogy is being made to understand what the author is intending to say through the figure of speech that he is using. When we apply this principle to our two texts, we find (as we would expect) that they are beautifully complementary.

You ask how at one and the same time the truth can be the foundation of the church and the church the foundation of the truth? Well, let me suggest the answer. What Paul is affirming in Ephesians 2:20 is that the church depends upon the truth for its existence. It rests upon the teaching of the apostles and the prophets, and without their teaching (now recorded in Scripture) the church could neither exist nor survive, let alone flourish. But according to 1 Timothy 3:15 the truth depends on the church for its defense and propagation. The church is called to serve the truth by holding it firm against attack, and by holding it high before the eyes of the world. Thus, the church *needs* the Bible because it is built on it. And the church *serves* the Bible by holding it fast and making it known. These are the two complementary truths that we are going to investigate further.

The church needs the Bible

The church's dependence on the Bible is manifold. Let me give you a number of examples.

a. The Bible created the church

Put thus baldly, this statement could be misleading. It could even be dismissed as inaccurate. For it is true that the Old Testament church as the people of God existed for centuries before the Bible was complete. Further, the New Testament church also existed for a long time before the New Testament canon was finalized, and longer still before the first Bible was printed for publication. Moreover, you may rightly say, the first-century church "shaped" the New Testament, in the sense that the Christian community shared in determining in what form the words and works of Jesus would be preserved for posterity. The church was thus the milieu with which the Bible came to be written and treasured. I agree with all these qualifications. Nevertheless, I repeat, the Bible may be said to have created the church. Or, more accurately, the Word of God (which is now written in the Bible) created the church. For how did the Christian church come into being? Answer: by the preaching of the apostles, who spoke not in the name of the church, but in the name of Christ.

On the day of Pentecost Peter added his apostolic testimony to the prophetic witness of the Old Testament, he proclaimed Jesus as Messiah and Lord, the Holy Spirit confirmed His words with power, and the believing people of God became the Spirit-filled Body of Christ. God Himself performed this creative work by His Spirit through His Word. Moreover He continued to honor the preaching of the apostles in the same way. On his famous missionary journeys Paul also bore witness to Christ, arguing that the testimony of the apostolic eyewitnesses was in full harmony with the Old Testament Scriptures. Many listened, repented, believed, and were baptized, so that churches were planted all over the Roman Empire. How? By the Word of God. God's Word (the combined witness of prophets and apostles), proclaimed in the power of the Spirit, created the church. It still does. The church is built on that foundation. And when the canon of the New Testament came to be determined, the church did not confer authority on these documents, but simply acknowledged the authority they already possessed. Why? Because they were "apostolic" and contained the teaching of the Lord's apostles.

For these reasons, we may truthfully say that the Bible (that is, the Word of God now written in the Bible) created and creates the church.

b. The Bible sustains the church

The Creator always sustains what He has created, and since He has brought the church into being, He keeps it in being. Moreover, having created it by His Word, He sustains and nourishes it by His Word. It is true, as Jesus said, quoting Deuteronomy (Matt. 4:4; cf. Deut. 8:3), that "man does not live on bread alone, but on every word that comes from the mouth of God," it is also true of churches. They cannot flourish without it. The church needs constantly to hear God's Word. Hence the central place of preaching in public worship. Preaching is not an intrusion into it but rather indispensable to it. For the worship of God is always a response to the Word of God. That is why, for example, in all the worship services of the Church of England, there is an oscillation between Word and worship. First God speaks His Word (in Scripture sentence, readings, and exposition), and then the people respond in confession, creed, praise, and prayer. The Christian congregation grows into maturity in Jesus Christ only as they hear, receive, believe, absorb, and obey the Word of God.

c. The Bible directs the church

The Christian community is a pilgrim people on its way to an eternal home. It is traveling through territory that is barren, pathless, hostile, and dark. It needs guidance for the way, and God has provided it.

"Your word is a lamp to my feet and a light for my path" (Ps. 119:105). I agree, of course, that what is called the "hermeneutical" task (that is, the task of interpreting the Scriptures) is difficult. Scripture does not give us slick answers to complex twentieth-century problems. We have to wrestle with the text, with both its meaning and its application, and do so in prayer, study, and fellowship with each other. Nevertheless, the principles we need to guide us are there in the Bible—theological and ethical principles—and together we can discover through the illumination of the Holy Spirit how to apply them to our lives in the contemporary world.

d. The Bible reforms the church

In every century, I am sorry to say, including our own, the church has deviated to some degree from God's truth and from His ethical standards. As Max Warren, the former missionary statesman, wrote in his book, *I Believe in the Great Commission*, church history is a "bittersweet story" in which the most outstanding fact is the infinite patience of God with His people. If then the church is constantly deviant, how can it be reformed? Answer: only by the Word of God. The greatest church renewal there has ever been in the history of the world was the sixteenth-century Reformation, and it was due, more than anything else, to the recovery of the Bible.

e. The Bible unites the church

Every Christian conscience should be troubled by the disunity of the church. I hope we have not grown accustomed to it or begun to acquiesce in it. The visible unity of the church (although we may not all agree with one another what precise form it should take) is surely a proper goal of Christian endeavor. What, then, is the basic reason for our continuing disunity? It is the lack of an agreed authority. So long as churches follow their own traditions and speculations, the universal church will continue to splinter. For example, the Anglican Church, to which I belong, is to blame in this matter. In its negotiations for unity or reunion, it insists on what it calls the "historic episcopate" as a non-negotiable item, and not only so, but often on a particular "catholic succession." Now all of us believe in *episkope* (the New Testament word for the pastoral oversight of the church). And a good historical, pastoral, and practical case can be made out for an episcopal form of government as being conducive to the well-being of the church. But it certainly cannot be made indispensable, for the simple reason that it is not required in Scripture. It can be defended as being consistent with biblical teaching and pastoral care. But that is another matter. In so far as the Church of England insists on it as non-negotiable, it is hindering the unity of the church. Once churches confess the supreme authority of Scripture, however, and its sole sufficiency for salvation, and are determined to judge their traditions by its teaching, then at once the way is opened for them to find unity in truth. The Bible unites the church when the church submits to it.

f. The Bible revives the church

We long for revival, for that special, unusual, supernatural visitation by God, as a result of which the whole community becomes aware of His living and holy presence. Sinners are convicted, penitents converted, backsliders restored, enemies reconciled, believers transformed, and dead churches revived. But how does revival happen? Only, it is true, by a sovereign work of the Holy Spirit of God. But what means does the Holy Spirit use? He uses His Word. The Word of God is "the sword of the Spirit" (Eph. 6:17; cf. Heb. 4:12), which He wields in His work in the world. Never separate the Spirit of God from the Word of God, for when the Holy Spirit uses this weapon in His sovereign power, He pricks the conscience, buts out cancerous growths from the body of Christ, and puts the devil to flight. It is the Bible that revives the church.

Are you convinced? I hope so. The church needs the Bible. The church depends on the Bible. The church is built upon the foundation of the apostles and prophets. The Bible is indispensable to the church's life, growth, nurture, direction, reformation, unity, and renewal. The church cannot exist without the Bible.

This leads to the second and complementary truth: if the church needs the Bible, the Bible also needs the church. If the church depends on the Bible, the Bible also depends on the church. For the church is called to serve the Bible by guarding and spreading its message.

The church serves the Bible

Although God spoke His Word through prophets and apostles, it had to be received and written down. Today it still needs to be translated, printed, published, distributed, preached, defended, broadcast, televised, and dramatized. In these and other ways the church is serving the Bible, guarding it and making it known.

This explains why Paul wrote in 1 Timothy 3:15 that the church is "the pillar and foundation of the truth." The two Greek words he used are instructive. The first is *stylos*, which undoubtedly means a pillar or column. The meaning of the other word *hedraioma* is not so certain and has been variously translated into English as "ground" (AV), "bulwark" (RSV), "buttress" (NEB) and "foundation" (NIV). It comes from the adjective *hedraios,* which means "firm, steady, stable," even "immovable" (it was used of mountains). So the noun *hedraioma* could be used of any kind of support or stabilizer. When applied to a building, therefore, it could refer either to its foundation or to a buttress, since the purpose of both is to keep the building stable.

Now let us put these two ideas together. The church is both the foundation or buttress of the truth, on the one hand, and the pillar of the truth, on the other. Foundations and buttresses hold a building firm; pillars hold it high, thrusting it aloft for people to see. This suggests respectively the apologetic task and the evangelistic task of the church. For as the foundation or buttress of the truth, the church must hold it firm and defend it against heretics, so that the truth remains steadfast and immovable. But, as the pillar of truth, the church must hold it high, making it visible to the world, so that people may see it and believe. So the Bible needs the church to protect it and to propagate it.

I am glad that the twentieth article of the Anglican Thirty-Nine Articles describes the church as "a witness and a keeper of Holy Writ." There is an urgent need for both these responsibilities. On the one hand, heresy is gaining ground in the church. There are false teachers who deny the infinite, loving personality of Almighty God, and others who deny the deity of our Lord Jesus Christ, as well as the authority of the Bible. These heretics seem to be increasing, and are spreading their pernicious ideas by books and sermons, on radio and television. So the truth needs buttresses—Christian scholars who will give their lives to what Paul called the defense and confirmation of the gospel (Phil. 1:7). Is God calling some younger theologian who is reading these words to be a buttress of the truth in the church, to hold it firm, to defend it against heresy and misunderstanding? What a vocation! The church must guard and demonstrate the truth.

At the same time, the church is called to preach the gospel throughout the world. There are some three hundred million people in the world who have never really heard of Jesus, and there are many more who, having heard of Him, have never believed in

Him. "How can they hear without someone preaching to them?" (Rom. 10:14). The church needs pioneer evangelists who will develop new forms of mission to penetrate closed areas, especially the Islamic, the Marxist, and the secular worlds. For the church is the pillar of the truth. So we've got to hold it high and make it known, so that people may see it in its beauty and adequacy, and embrace it for themselves.

Conclusion

The church needs the Bible and the Bible needs the church. Those are the complementary truths that Paul's two statements express. The church could not survive without the Bible to sustain it, and the Bible could hardly survive without the church to guard and spread it. Each needs the other. The Bible and the church are twins, inseparable, Siamese twins. Once we have got hold of that, we are ready for a threefold exhortation.

First, I exhort Christian pastors (including myself) to take our preaching more seriously. Our calling is to study and expound the Word of God, relate it to the modern world. The health of every congregation depends more than anything else on the quality of its preaching ministry. This may surprise you. I know, of course, that church members can grow into maturity in Christ in spite of their pastors, and even when their pastors are bad and neglectful. For they can pray and read the Scriptures both by themselves and in fellowship groups, and nowadays good books and cassettes are available as a valuable supplementary means of instruction. Nevertheless, the New Testament indicates that God's purpose is to commit the care of His people to pastors, who are so to proclaim Christ to them out of the Scriptures, in the glory of His person and work, that their worship, faith, and obedience are drawn out from them. That is why I dare to say that, more often than not, the pew is a reflection of the pulpit, and that the pew does not normally rise higher than the pulpit. So then, my fellow pastors, let us determine afresh to give ourselves to this priority task!

Second, I exhort Christian people, not only to study the Bible yourselves in your home and in your fellowship group, but to demand (it is not too strong a word) faithful, biblical preaching from your pastors. Let me put it like this: The ministry you get is the ministry you deserve, and the ministry you deserve is the ministry you demand! Lay people have much more power in the churches than they commonly realize. They join a church where the Bible is hardly ever preached and give in to it, acquiesce in it, do nothing about it! There may be times when you need to have the courage to reprove your pastors because you perceive that they are not being diligent in their study and faithful in their exposition. But don't give us only your reproof; give us your encouragement and your prayers. Set your pastors free from the distracting burden of administration. Pastoral oversight should also be shared by the lay leaders of the congregation. Every generation needs to relearn the lesson of Acts 6, where the apostles refused to be deflected from the teaching role to which Christ had called them. They delegated certain social and administrative tasks to devote themselves "to prayer and to the ministry of the word" (Acts 6:1ff). It is the lay leaders of the congregation who can ensure that the same priority is recognized today.

Third, I want to exhort Christian parents. Teach the Bible to your children. Don't surrender this parental responsibility to the church, even, or to the school; do it yourselves, so that your children, like Timothy, come to know the Holy Scriptures from childhood (2 Tim. 3:15). If you do this, then the next generation of church leaders that arises will grasp, as the present generation doesn't seem to, the indispensable place of the Bible in the church.

So let us enthrone the Bible in the home and in the church, not because we worship it but because God speaks through it. Then, as we hear His voice again, the church will be renewed, reformed, and revived, and will become what God has always intended it to be—a bright light shining in the prevailing darkness.

5. The Christian and the Bible

Let me rehearse briefly the territory that we have traversed. We have thought about "God and the Bible" because He is its author, about "Christ and the Bible" because He is its subject, about the "Holy Spirit and the Bible" because He was the means of its inspiration, and about the "church and the Bible" because the church is built upon it and is called to guard its treasures and make them known. We conclude with something more personal and individual—"The Christian and the Bible."

I do not hesitate to say that the Bible is indispensable to every Christian's health and growth. Christians who neglect the Bible simply do not mature. When Jesus quoted from Deuteronomy to the effect that human beings do not live by bread only but by God's Word, He was asserting that the Word of God is just as necessary for spiritual health as food is for bodily health. I am not now thinking of remote Christian tribespeople into whose language the Bible has not yet been translated, nor of illiterate people who may have the Bible in their language but are unable to read it for themselves. To be sure, such people are not altogether cut off from the nourishment of God's Word, for they can still receive it, though at one or two removes, from a missionary, pastor, relative, or friend. I am bound to say, however, that I think their Christian life would be enriched if they could have direct access to the Scriptures, which is why such heroic work has been done to have the Bible translated into the languages of the world. I am not thinking of these situations. I am thinking rather about ourselves. We have a plethora of Bibles in a variety of editions and versions. Our problem is not that the Bible is unavailable to us, but that we do not take advantage of its availability. We need to read and meditate on it daily, to study it in a fellowship group and to hear it expounded during Sunday worship. Otherwise, we shall not grow. Growth into maturity in Christ depends upon a close acquaintance with, and a believing response to, the Bible.

I want to try to answer the question that may be forming in your minds: Just how and why does the Bible enable us to grow? As an illustration of its effectiveness as a means of grace I have chosen the story of Jesus' washing of His apostles' feet, recorded in John 13. When He had finished, put on His outer garment again, and returned to His place, He immediately referred to Himself as their teacher: "You call me 'Teacher' and 'Lord', and rightly so, for that is what I am" (v. 13). The implication is clear that through His act of foot-washing He had been teaching them certain truths and lessons that He wanted them to learn. There seem to have been three.

a. He was teaching them about Himself

Jesus' actions were a deliberate parable of His mission. John seems clearly to have understood this, for he introduces the incident with these words: "Jesus, knew . . . that he had come from God and was returning to God: so he got up from the meal . . . " (vv. 3-4). That is, knowing these things, He dramatized them in action. Perhaps the best commentary is Philippians 2, which unfolds the stages of His self-humbling before He was highly exalted. Thus Jesus "got up from the meal" as He had risen from His heavenly throne. He "took off his outer clothing" as He had laid aside His glory and emptied Himself of it. He then "wrapped a towel around his waist" (the badge of servitude) as in the incarnation He had taken the form of a servant. Next, He began "to wash his disciples' feet, drying them with the towel" as He went to the cross to secure our cleansing from sin. After this He "put on his clothes and returned to his place" as He returned to His heavenly glory and sat down at the Father's right hand. By these actions, He was dramatizing His whole earthly career. He was teaching them about Himself, who He was, where He had come from, and where He was going.

b. He was teaching them about His salvation
He said to Peter, "Unless I wash you, you have no part with me" (v. 8). In other words, the forgiveness of sin is a necessary prelude to fellowship with Jesus Christ. Until and unless we have been washed, we cannot have anything to do with Him. More subtly still, Jesus distinguished between two different kinds of washing: the bath and the washing of feet. The apostles were familiar with this social distinction. Before visiting a friend's home, they would take a bath. Then on arrival at their friend's a servant would wash their feet. They wouldn't need another bath, but only a foot-washing. Jesus seems to have used this well-known cultural distinction to teach a less well-known theological distinction: When we first come to Him in penitence and faith we get a bath and are washed all over. Theologically, it is called "justification" or "regeneration," and is symbolized in baptism. Then, when we fall into sin as Christians, what we need is not another bath (we cannot be rejustified or rebaptized) but a foot-washing; that is, the cleansing of a daily forgiveness. So Jesus says in verse 10, "A person who has had a bath needs only to wash his feet; his whole body is clean."

c. He was teaching them about His will
We know from the Synoptic Gospels that before sitting down for the meal in the upper room the apostles had been squabbling about who was to have the best seats. They were so preoccupied with questions of precedence that they sat down to the

meal unwashed. Evidently there had been no servant to wash their feet, and it hadn't occurred to them that one of them might assume that lowly role and wash the feet of the others. So during supper Jesus did what none of them would have demeaned himself to do. When He finished, He said to them, "Now that I, your Lord and Teacher, have washed your feet, you also should wash one another's feet. I have set you an example that you should do as I have done for you. I tell you the truth, no servant is greater than his master. . . . Now that you know these things, you will be blessed if you do them" (vv. 14-17). Our Lord stooped to serve. It is His will that we do so too.

Here, then, were Jesus' three lessons from one incident: first about His person (that He had come from God and was going to God), second about His salvation (that after the bath of justification we need only the continuous washing of our feet), and third about His will (that we must wash one another's feet, that is, express our love for one another in humble service). Or, put another way, He taught three lessons that required three responses. In giving them a revelation of Himself, He was asking for their worship. In giving them a promise of salvation, He was asking for their trust. In giving them a commandment to love and serve one another, He was asking for their obedience.

I do not think it an exaggeration to claim that all the teaching of the Bible can be divided into these three categories, requiring these three responses. For throughout Scripture there are revelations of God demanding our worship, promises of salvation demanding our faith, and commandments about our duty demanding our obedience. Having considered the foot-washing as one example, let us look at this threefold pattern a little more fully.

Revelations of God

The Bible is God's self-disclosure, the divine autobiography. In the Bible the subject and the object are identical, for in it God is speaking about God. He makes Himself known progressively in the rich variety of His Being: as the Creator of the universe and of human beings in His own image, the climax of His creation; as the living God who sustains and animates everything He has made; as the covenant God who chose Abraham, Isaac, Jacob, and their descendants to be His special people; and as a gracious God who is slow to anger and quick to forgive, but also as a righteous God who punishes idolatry and injustice among His own people as well as in pagan nations. Then in the New Testament He reveals Himself as the Father of our Lord and Savior Jesus Christ, who sent Him into the world to take our nature upon Him, to be born and grow, live and teach, work and suffer, die and rise, occupy the throne and send the Holy Spirit; next as the God of the new covenant community, the church, who sends His people into the world as His witnesses and His servants in the power of the Holy Spirit; and finally as the God who one day will send Jesus Christ in power and glory to save, to judge, and to reign, who will create a new universe, and who in the end will be everything to everybody.

This majestic revelation of God (Father, Son, and Holy Spirit), which unfolds from the creation to the consummation, moves us to worship. When we catch these glimpses of the greatness of God, of His glory and grace, we fall down on our faces before Him and bring to Him the homage of our lips, our hearts, and our lives. It is impossible to read the Bible with any sensitivity and not be a worshiper. The Word of God evokes the worship of God.

Promises of salvation

We have already seen that God's main purpose in giving us the Bible is to make us "wise for salvation through faith in Christ Jesus" (2 Tim. 3:15). So the Bible tells the story of Jesus, foretelling and foreshadowing Him in the Old Testament, describing His earthly career in the Gospels, and unfolding in the Epistles the fullness of His person and work. More than that, the Scripture does not just present Jesus to us as our all-sufficient Savior; it urges us to go to Him and put our trust in Him. And it promises us that, if we do so, we shall receive the forgiveness of our sins and the gift of the liberating Holy Spirit. The Bible is full of salvation promises. It pledges new life in the new community to those who respond to the call of Jesus Christ. Jesus gave one such promise to Peter in the incident of the foot-washing when He said to him, "You are clean" (John 13:10). Peter's mind must often have grasped that promise and believed it. Even after he had denied Jesus, he was not repudiated. Of course he needed to repent, to be forgiven, to be recommissioned. But he did not need another bath, since already he had been made clean. The words of Jesus must have reassured his heart and pacified his nagging conscience.

Do you remember how in *Pilgrim's Progress*, after the disastrous experience in Bypath Meadow, Christian and Hopeful found themselves in the grounds of Doubting Castle? Its owner was Giant Despair, who found them asleep when they should have been praying. He then "put them into his castle," writes Bunyan, "in a very dark dungeon, nasty and stinking to the spirits of these two men. Here, then, they lay from Wednesday morning till Saturday night, without one bit of bread, or drop of drink, or light, or any to ask them how they did." In the morning at his wife's instigation, Giant took "a grievous crab-tree cudgel," and "fell upon them and beat them fearfully"—with doubts, of course. The next day, his wife advised him "to counsel them to make away with themselves," which Giant did, "either with knife, halter or poison." That is, since they were never likely to escape, they might as well take their own lives. Giant Despair is always whispering to his victims about suicide. On the third day he took them into the castle yard and showed them "the bones and skulls" of their predecessors. "These," he said with glee, "were pilgrims, as you are, once, and they trespassed on my grounds, as you have done; and when I saw fit, I tore them in pieces; and so within ten days I will do to you. Get you to your den again . . . ."

All that day Christian and Hopeful lay there, says Bunyan, "in a lamentable case, as before." There seemed no possibility of escape. Then at about midnight "they began to pray, and continued in prayer till almost break of day." A little before then Christian "brake out into this passionate speech: What a fool, quoth he, am I, thus to lie in a stinking dungeon, when I may as well walk in liberty! I have a key in my bosom called Promise that will, I am persuaded, open any lock in Doubting Castle. Then said Hopeful, That's good news, good brother, pluck it out of thy bosom, and try." So he did, and "the door flew open with ease"—then the outward door, and then the iron gate, and they escaped with speed. Awakened by the creaking of the gate, Giant rose to pursue them, but he "felt his limbs to fail, for his fits took him again, so that he could by no means go after them."

You too have a key in your bosom called Promise, for God has given it to you in the Scriptures. Have you ever used it to escape from Doubting Castle? When Satan harasses our conscience, and tries to persuade us that there is not forgiveness for such sinners as we are, only a trustful reliance on God's promises to the penitent can liberate us from his harassment. We have to learn to rest in perplexity on the promise of His guidance, in fear on the promise of His protection, in loneliness on the promise of His presence. The promises of God can garrison our hearts and minds, His promises of salvation.

It is in this connection that I think I should refer to the two gospel sacraments, baptism and the Lord's supper. Although Protestants have different ways of formulating their understanding of these ordinances, we should be able to accept the dictum from the Second Book of Homilies (1571) that they are "visible signs to which are annexed promises." That the water of baptism and the bread and wine of communion are "outward and visible signs" is obvious. More particularly, however, they are signs of God's grace, signs that visibly promise His cleansing, forgiveness, and new life to those who repent and believe in Jesus. So they elicit and strengthen our faith.

Commandments to obey

In calling out a people for Himself, God told them what kind of people He wanted them to be. They were a special people; He expected from them special conduct. So He gave them the Ten Commandments as a summary of His will, which Jesus underlined in His Sermon on the Mount, uncovering their disturbing implications. The righteousness of His disciples, He said, must "surpass" the righteousness of the scribes and Pharisees (Matt. 5:20). It would be "greater" in the sense that it would be deeper, a righteousness of the heart, a glad and radical inward obedience.

It is particularly important in our day to emphasize God's call to moral obedience, because at least two groups of people are denying it. First, there are the advocates of the so-called "New Morality" or "Situation Ethics," developed in the 1960s. They argue that God's one and only absolute command is love, that all other laws have been abrogated, and that love is by itself a sufficient guide to Christian conduct. Whatever is expressive of love is good, they say; whatever is incompatible with it is evil. Now certainly true love (the sacrifice of self in service of others) is the preeminent Christian virtue, and to follow its dictates is extremely demanding. Nevertheless, love needs guidelines, and it is the direction that God's commandments supply. Love does not dispense with law; it fulfills it (Rom. 13:8-10).

Second, there are evangelical Christians who interpret Paul's assertions that "Christ is the end of the law" (Rom. 10:4) and that "you are not under law, but under grace" (Rom. 6:14) as meaning that Christians are no longer under obligation to obey God's moral law. To try to do so, they say, is a "legalism" that contradicts the freedom Christ has given us. But they misunderstand Paul. The "legalism" Paul rejected was not obedience to God's law in itself, but the attempt by such obedience to win God's favor and forgiveness. This is impossible, he wrote, for "no one will be declared righteous in his sight by observing the law" (Rom. 3:20).

Once justified by God's sheer grace, however,

that is, declared righteous in His sight by His free and undeserved favor through Christ, we are then under obligation to keep His law, and want to do so. Indeed, Christ died for us precisely "in order that the righteous requirements of the law might be fully met in us" (Rom. 8:3-4), and God puts His Spirit in our hearts to write His law there (Jer. 31:33; Ezek. 36:27; Gal. 5:22-23). Our Christian freedom, therefore, is freedom to obey, not to disobey. As Jesus said several times, if we love Him we shall keep His commandments (John 14:15, 21-24; 15:14). And it is in Scripture that God's commandments are to be found.

Thus, in the Bible God gives us revelations of Himself, which lead us to worship; promises of salvation, which stimulate our faith; and commandments expressing His will, which demand our obedience. This is the meaning of Christian discipleship. Its three essential ingredients are worship, faith, and obedience. And all three are called forth by the Word of God. Worship is the response to God's self-revelation. It is an adoring preoccupation with the glory of God, and, as William Sangster once put it, it can "disinfect us of egoism." Faith is a restful confidence in the promises of God. It delivers us from the see-saw of religious experience—up and down, up and down, Sunday night, Monday morning. Nothing can deliver us from that but the promises of God. For our feelings fluctuate, whereas God's Word remains forever firm. Obedience is a loving commitment to the will of God. It rescues us from the bog of moral relativism and sets our feet upon the rock of

The Christian and the Bible

God's absolute commands.

Moreover, worship, faith, and obedience—the three ingredients of discipleship—are all outward-looking. In worship we are preoccupied with God's glory, in faith with His promises, in obedience with His commands. Authentic Christian discipleship is never introverted. The Bible is a marvelously liberating book. It pulls us out of ourselves and makes us instead obsessed with God, His glory, promises, and will. To love God thus (and to love others for His sake) is to be set free from the tyrannous bondage of our own self-centeredness. The Christian who is engrossed in himself becomes as paralyzed as the self-conscious centipede in the humorous modern parable:

> The centipede was happy quite
> Until a toad in fun
> Exclaimed "which leg comes after which?"
> This put his mind in such a pitch
> He lay distracted in the ditch
> Considering how to run!
>
> While lying in this sorry plight
> A ray of sunshine caught his sight
> And bursting into happy song
> Unthinking he began to run
> And quite forgot the croaker's fun.

Only rays of light from God's Word, which lift our eyes to Him, can deliver us from the paralysis that comes from self-preoccupation.

Conclusion

The vital place of the Bible in the Christian life exposes the extreme gravity of liberal theology. By undermining public confidence in the reliability of the Bible, it makes Christian discipleship all but impossible. Let me explain. All Christians agree that discipleship includes worship, faith, and obedience. Worship, faith, and obedience are essential parts of our Christian life. We cannot live as Christians without them. Yet none is possible without a reliable Bible.

How can we worship God if we don't know who He is, what He is like, or what kind of worship is pleasing to Him? Christians are not Athenians who worship an unknown God. We must know God before we can worship Him. And it is the Bible that tells us what He is like.

Again, how can we believe or trust in God if we don't know His promises? Faith is not a synonym for superstition, or another word for credulity. Faith is a reasoning trust. It rests on the promises of God and on the character of the God who made them. Without promises our faith shrivels up and dies. And God's promises are found in the Bible.

Again, how can we obey God, if we don't know His will and commandments? Christian obedience is not blind obedience, but open-eyed and loving. For God has given us commandments in the Bible, and shown us that they are not burdensome.

So then, without God's revelation worship is impossible; without God's promises faith is impossible;

without God's commandments obedience is impossible. Therefore without the Bible discipleship is impossible.

Do we realize how blessed we are to have a Bible in our hands? God has graciously made provision for our discipleship. He has revealed to us Himself, His salvation, and His will. He has made it possible for us to worship Him, trust Him, and obey Him, in other words, to live as His loving children in the world.

We need then to come expectantly to the Bible each day. The great curse of our Bible reading, whenever it becomes just a stale and boring routine, is that we do not come to it expectantly. We don't come with confidence that God is willing, able, and anxious to speak to us through His Word. We need to come to the Bible every day with the petition of Samuel on our lips, "Master, speak, your servant is listening." And He will! Sometimes through His Word He will give us a revelation of Himself; we shall perceive something of His glory; our heart will be deeply moved within us; and we shall fall down and worship Him. Sometimes through His word He will give us a promise; we shall grasp it, lay hold of it, and say, "Lord, I'm not going to let it go until I inherit it, and until it becomes true of me." Sometimes through the Bible He will give us a command; we shall see our need to repent of our disobedience; and we shall pray and resolve that by His grace we shall obey it in years to come.

These revelations, promises, and commandments we shall store up in our mind until our Christian memory becomes like a well-stocked cupboard. Then from its shelves in moments of need we shall be able to take down truths or promises or commandments that are appropriate to the situation in which we find ourselves. Without this, we condemn ourselves to perpetual immaturity. Only if we meditate on the Word of God, listen to God speaking to us, hear His voice, and respond to Him in worship, faith, and obedience will we grow into maturity in Christ.

Postscript

I have been concerned in this little book both about the Bible's "yesterday" (its historical origins) and about its "today" (its contemporary relevance). I have tried to develop a simple, Trinitarian doctrine of Scripture as a message that comes from God (He spoke it and speaks it), focuses on Christ (He witnesses to it as witnessing to Him), and was articulated by the Holy Spirit through the human authors (so that His words and theirs coincided). The practical usefulness of the Bible today, both for the church and for the individual Christian, depends on our acceptance of its divine origin and purpose. Paul himself combined these things when he described all Scripture as being on the one hand "God-breathed" and on the other "useful" (2 Tim. 3:16-17). It is useful for us ("for teaching, rebuking, correcting and training in righteousness"), precisely because it was breathed out of the mouth of God. So our view and our use of the Bible go together. It matters what we think about it.

I, for one, deeply disturbed by the cavalier attitude to the Bible adopted by many, long to see it reinstated in the hearts and homes of Christian people, and enthroned in the pulpits of the world. Only then can the church again hear and heed God's Word. Only then will God's people learn to integrate their faith and their life, as they seek to apply the teaching of Scripture to their moral standards, economic lifestyle, marriage and family, work and citizenship. Only then can Christians hope to be the world's salt and light, as Jesus said they were to be, and influence their country's culture, its institutions and laws, its values and ideals.

The practical usefuless of Scripture—for church and Christian, home and nation—should not, however, be our main reason for desiring its reinstatement, but rather the glory of God. If the Bible might rightly be called "the Word of God" (though spoken through the words of men), then clearly to neglect it is to neglect Him, while to listen to it is to listen to Him. The overriding reason to "let the word of Christ dwell in you richly" (Col. 3:16) is not that we shall thereby be enriched, but that He will thereby be honored and glorified. He wants us to have a Christian mind as well as to live a Christian life. But to have a Christian mind we must have His mind, "the mind of Christ" (cf. 1 Cor. 2:16; Phil. 2:5). And our mind can be conformed to His mind only as it becomes soaked in His Word. That is why *the Bible* is the *book for today.*

Note to the Reader

The publisher invites you to share your response to the message of this book by writing Discovery House Publishers, P.O. Box 3566, Grand Rapids, MI 49501, U.S.A. or by calling 1-800-283-8333. For information about other Discovery House publications, contact us at the same address and phone number.